To *Moroni*
With Love

TO MORONI WITH LOVE
by ED DECKER
ISBN# 1-60039-179-6

Pubished by LAMP POST INC.
www.lamppostpubs.com

A Publication of
Saints Alive In Jesus
P.O. Box 1347
Issaquah, WA 98027
USA
ed@SaintsAlive.com
www.SaintsAlive.com

Cover design by
Michelle De Monnin for
De Monnin's Art Studio

Unless otherwise indicated,
all Scripture quotations are
taken from The King James
Version of the Bible.

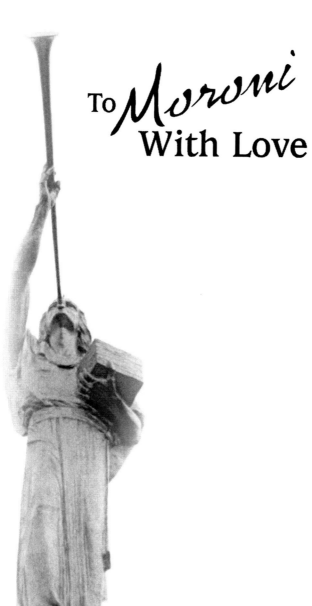

To *Moroni*
With Love

by ED DECKER

DEDICATION

I dedicate this book to my hero in the faith, the Late Dr. Walter Martin, the greatest Christian Apologist of the 20th Century, who helped me work my way out of Mormonism. He became my good friend, my inspiration, my challenger and my encourager.

I would like to encourage you to visit Dr. Walter Martin's official website at www.WalterMartin.com.

THE CHALLENGE

THIS IS A VERY SPECIAL BOOK. I'm sure that you have never read one quite like it. And I can assure you that it has been a tremendous burden of research and prayer for me in its development. It is given to you, my LDS friend, in love and in Christ.

If you are a member of the Church of Jesus Christ of Latter-day Saints, you may doubt the sincerity of that love, but I assure you that it is real and it is honest. If you are one of the many people investigating the church, I pray that you will take time out from your studies to read this thoroughly and ask the Lord to settle the matter in your heart and mind.

Whatever your reason for reading these words, I promise that the next hour of reading time may well be the most significant hour in your spiritual life. Significant, because it will either solidify your belief in the absolute truth of the Mormon message, or questions will be raised that may cause you to take another and deeper look at some of the key doctrines of the church.

I write this an ex-Mormon who spent almost 20 years in the LDS Church, a member of the Melchizedek priesthood, a Temple Mormon and active in many church callings. I am setting forth a challenge that first came from Brigham Young:

> Take up the Bible, compare the religion of the Latter-day Saints with it and see if it will stand the test. *(Journal of Discourses 16:46, 1873)*

> No man can disprove a truth...Why not rather every man rise up and say, "Let God be true, let the truth remain and let me know the truth. That is what I want I will submit to it; and let every false theory and principle fall, to rise up no more." *(ibid. 8:132, 1860.)*

Even more to the point was Orson Pratt's statement regarding the "truth":

> If we cannot convince you by reason nor by the Word of God, that your religion is wrong, we will not persecute you...we ask of you the same generosity...Convince us

of our errors of doctrine, if we have any, by logical argu-
ments, or by the Word of God and we will be ever grateful
for the information, and you will ever have the pleasing
reflections that you have been instruments in the hands of
God of redeeming your fellow beings. *(The Seer, p.15)*

I am not going to try to outwit or out quote Mormon theo-
logians and apologists. I am just going to tell it to you like it is,
and put the "Restored Gospel" of the LDS Church to the test of
God's Word and common sense logic.

MY CHALLENGE is that you read this with the same sincere heart mentioned in Moroni 10:4, asking God to manifest
His truth to you. I exhort you to apply the same test to these
pages. Seek not my truth or the Mormon truth, but **God's eternal truth**. Our very eternal lives are at stake, both yours and
mine.

It is my solemn witness before God that he hold me
accountable for any soul that I might lead from the light of
His Son Jesus into the darkness of error and false doctrine.
It is my earnest prayer that God so bless each reader with a
full comprehension of the information written herein that,
through His Holy Spirit, the truth will be evidenced without
doubt or turmoil.

POINTS OF REFERENCE

IT IS THE PREMISE OF THIS work that the Mormon and the
Christian worship at entirely different altars, with "gospels"
that fully separate the one from the other. It is therefore quite
important that we identify the major points of division so that
we can work from correct points of reference.

JOSEPH SMITH'S FIRST VISION

One of the most important events in all of Mormon history
was the day that God the Father and Jesus Christ came down,
in the flesh, and told Joseph Smith that the churches were all
wrong and that, in effect, Christianity was totally lost.

> When the Light rested upon me I saw two personages...
> one of them spake unto me, calling me by name and said,
> pointing to the other, "This is My beloved Son, hear Him!"
> I asked the Personages who stood above me in the light
> which of all the sects was right and which I should join.
> I was answered that I must join none of them, for they
> were all wrong...all their creeds were an abomination in
> His sight, that those professors were all corrupt. *(Pearl of
> Great Price, Joseph Smith, History 1:19)*

CHRISTIANITY LOST

If we accept Joseph Smith's word for this, we must immediately conclude the Christian church is in very deep trouble. While the Christian may doubt the authenticity of Joseph Smith's statements, several very solid facts remain.

<u>First</u>, it is the basic Mormon belief that God finds the Christian worship of Him unacceptable and even loathsome.

<u>Second</u>, the LDS belief in a great apostasy irrevocably separates Mormonism and Christianity.

<u>Third</u>, there is no way that both can be right. The claims of Mormonism to being the "restored" church exclude that possibility forever.

THE NATURE OF THE MORMON GOD

The foregoing description of God's appearance to Joseph Smith is noteworthy beyond his expressed displeasure with Christianity. Far more critical is his statement that God the Father *and* Jesus Christ both appeared before him separately, side by side, and in the flesh. It is critical because it immediately separates Mormonism and Christianity in regard to the nature of God.

Deeper review of the LDS doctrine of the Godhead reveals further separation. Basically, it is found in the doctrine of the "Law of Eternal Progression" (as man is, God once was as God is, man may become). In the book *Mormon Doctrine*, we are told:

> Further, as the Prophet also taught, there is a God above the Father of our Lord Jesus Christ...**God the Father of Jesus Christ had a father**...Mortal persons who overcome all things and gain an ultimate exaltation will live eternally in the family unit and have spirit children, thus becoming eternal Fathers and eternal Mothers. God Himself, the Father of us all, is a glorified, exalted immortal resurrected man. *(Mormon Doctrine, Bruce R. McConkie, pp.322-23, 517, 643)*

Joseph Smith really let the cat out of the bag in his sermon at the funeral of King Follett. Because of the length of the sermon, I will extract a few of the key thoughts.

> I will prove that the world is wrong by showing what God is...I will go back to the beginning before the world was... God Himself was once as we are now and is an exalted man and sits enthroned in yonder heavens. That is the Great Secret. We have imagined and supposed that God was God from all eternity. I will refute that idea...

> Here then is eternal life to know the only true God; and you have got to learn to be Gods yourselves, and to be kings and priests to God, the same as all Gods have done before you namely by going from one small degree to another from grace to grace, from exaltation to exaltation...and to sit in glory as do all those who sit, enthroned in everlasting power. *(Teachings of the Prophet Joseph Smith, p.345 -47)*

Not only did he tear apart the Christian belief about the nature of God, but he then brought to full circle the Law of Eternal Progression by placing man within it.

Putting all this into perspective, Joseph Smith then described the method by which his God planned the creation of the world.

> In the beginning, the head of the Gods called a council of the Gods; and they came together and concocted a plan to create the world and people it. *(ibid. p.349)*

BIBLICAL PERSPECTIVE ON GOD

The Biblical position on this is quite simple. It just doesn't teach or accept a single part of the "Law of Eternal Progression." The Bible is very clear in the matter.

> I am He, before me there was no God formed, neither shall there be any after me. I, even I, am the Lord; and beside me there is no Saviour. (Isaiah 43:10-11)

> I am the first, and I am the last; and beside me there is no God. (Isaiah 44:6)

> God is a Spirit and they that worship Him must worship Him in spirit and in truth. (John 4:24)

> For when God made promise to Abraham, because He could swear by no greater, He swore by Himself. (Hebrews 6:13)

> No man hath seen God at any time; the only begotten Son, which is in the bosom of the Gather, He hath declared Him. (John 1:18)

> God is not a man, that He should lie; neither the son of man that he should repent. (Numbers 23:19)

On these and many other scriptures like them, stands the Biblical concept of God. They are in total disagreement with the Mormon view.

In fact, the whole matter goes beyond the concept of "different views of God"; we are dealing with "views of different Gods!" The emphasis is critical.

What we face is the fact that either Mormonism is correct or the Bible is correct. One is right, the other is wrong!

THE TWO KINDS OF MORMON SALVATION

Articles 2 and 3 of the Articles of Faith of the LDS church give a brief look into Mormon doctrines regarding salvation.

> We believe that men shall be punished for their own sins and not for Adam's transgression.

> We believe that through the Atonement of Christ, all mankind may be saved, by obedience to the Laws and Ordinances of the Gospel. [the LDS Gospel]

The LDS gospel essentially teaches that everyone will be saved. But the *degree of glory* depends on one's obedience to the Mormon doctrine, including everything from tithing to Temple Ordinances for self and family, as well as baptism for the dead, obedience to the living Prophet and the hierarchy of the Priesthood, attending all meetings, missionary work, welfare work, etc. Perhaps the most widely accepted work on the subject is *The Articles of Faith* by James Talmage.

The summation of his words is the LDS position that there are actually two levels of salvation.

LEVEL 1—THE GENERAL SALVATION

Talmage explains it this way:

> The extent of the atonement is universal, applying alike to all descendants of Adam. Even the unbeliever, the heathen and the child who dies before reaching the years of discretion, all are redeemed by the Saviour's self-sacrifice from the individual consequences of the fall. *(Articles of Faith, p.85)*

In other words, Christ's death upon the cross brought a general salvation for all men, which is a resurrection in order to be judged for our works.

LEVEL 2—INDIVIDUAL SALVATION, OR EXALTATION

> Of the Saved, not all will be exalted to the higher glories. No one can be admitted to any order of glory, in short, no soul can be saved until Justice has been satisfied for violated law...In the Kingdom of God there are numerous levels of gradations provided for those who are worthy of them. *(ibid. p.91)*

The basic LDS doctrine is that Christ's atonement places all humanity at a judgment table to be reviewed for our righteousness and works, or "obedience to the laws and ordinances of the gospel."

The LDS concept is, we shall all have access to 3 different kingdoms of levels of glory, depending upon our worthiness. The lake of fire, as a place of destination, is not part of present-day LDS theology.

The **Celestial Kingdom**, the highest level of which is reserved for those obedient members of the Melchizedek Priesthood, who shall, with their worthy wives, become gods and goddesses.

The **Terrestrial Kingdom** is a secondary level set aside for those who, though honorable, failed to comply with the requirements for exaltation, or for those who proved not valiant in the testimony of Jesus Christ.

The **Telestial Kingdom** is the lowest. It is reserved for those who had no testimony of the gospel and were lost in the carnality of the world.

THE CHRISTIAN CONCEPT OF SALVATION

In contrast, the Christian understanding of salvation is altogether different. In the first place, the Bible teaches that all humanity has sinned and faces the judgment of God.

> *All have sinned and come short of the glory of God. (Romans 3:23)*

> *The soul that sinneth, it shall die. (Ezekiel 18:20)*

> *And whosoever was not found written in the book of life was cast into the lake of fire. (Revelation 20:15)*

But the Bible also teaches that God has provided a way to forgiveness and eternal life for man. It is not something we can do. It is something God has already done for us! It can be summed up in one scripture:

> *For God so loved the world, that he gave his only begotten Son, that whosoever believeth in him should not perish, but have everlasting life. (John 3:16)*

The Bible teaches that it is only through Christ that a person can be forgiven of sin and released from its penalties.

> For he hath made him to be sin for us, who knew no sin; that we might be made the righteousness of God in him. (2 Corinthians 5:21)

> For the wages of sin is death; but the gift of God is eternal life through Jesus Christ our Lord. (Romans 6:23)

The Bible teaches that salvation is a free gift, price already paid, unearned by us.

> For by grace are ye saved through faith; and that not of yourselves: it is the gift of God: Not of works, lest any man should boast. (Ephesians 2:8-9)

> I do not frustrate the grace of God: for if righteousness come by the law, then Christ is dead in vain. (Galatians 2:21)

> Wherefore the law was our schoolmaster to bring us unto Christ, that we might be justified by faith. (Galatians 3:24)

The Bible teaches that by confessing and forsaking our sins, asking the Lord to forgive us, confessing our inability to come to the Father except through Jesus and asking Him to be our Saviour and Lord of our life, we shall be forgiven and be born-again and live eternally with God.

> Whosoever therefore shall confess me before men, him will I confess also before my Father which is in heaven. (Matthew 10:32)

> I am the way, the truth, and the life; no man cometh unto the Father, but by me. (John 14:6)

The Bible also teaches that those who refuse to believe Christ and obey Him will experience frightful judgment by God. Read Revelation 20:11-15. There are no three levels of glory taught here but the lake of fire! Also, John 3:36 states:

> He that believeth on the Son hath everlasting life: and he that believeth not the Son shall not see life; but the wrath of God abideth on him.

IN COMPARISON

THE DIFFERENCE BETWEEN THE TWO THEOLOGIES is this: The Mormon believes that personal salvation is a function or result of works of righteousness and obedience to laws and ordinances of the gospel.

The Bible teaches that works and obedience to God's laws are a function or *result* of personal salvation.

In other words, the Bible teaches that you don't bark to become a dog, you bark because you are one. You can sit there forever and go "Baa, Baa, Baa" but you will never become a sheep. You bark because you ARE a dog, you baa because you ARE a sheep. You don't work to get saved; you work because and when you ARE saved.

The scriptures say it this way:

> But Israel, which followed after the law of righteousness, hath not attained to the law of righteousness. Wherefore? Because they sought it not by faith, but as it were by the works of the law. For they stumbled at that stumbling stone. *(Romans 9:31-32)*

> Brethren, my heart's desire and prayer to God for Israel is, that they might be saved. For I bear them record that they have a zeal of God, but not according to knowledge. For they being ignorant of God's righteousness, and going about to establish their own righteousness, have not submitted themselves unto the righteousness of God. For Christ is the end of the law for righteousness to every one that believeth. *(Romans 10:1-4)*

Either the Mormon concept of salvation is correct or the Biblical concept of salvation is correct. One is **RIGHT** and the other is **WRONG!**

NEW SCRIPTURE

Another point of separation between Mormonism and Christianity is the LDS belief that God has revealed, through His Latter-day Prophet, new and more complete scripture. The LDS Church teaches that *The Book of Mormon*, *The Pearl of Great Price*, and *Doctrine and Covenants* are all new and vital scripture.

The Christian denies the divine origin of these and

maintains the Holy Bible to be the only Holy Scripture given by God.

> *Ye shall not add unto the Word which I command you, neither shall ye diminish ought from it, that ye may keep the commandments of the LORD your God, which I command you. (Deuteronomy 4:2)*

> *What thing soever I command you observe to do it; thou shalt not add thereto, nor diminish it. (Deuteronomy 12:32)*

> *Add thou not unto His words, lest He reprove thee, and thou be found a liar. (Proverbs 30:6)*

Thus, the Bible shows the LDS scriptures false. Again, either the Mormons are correct in this or the Christians. There can be no middle of the road.

WHAT'S THE DIFFERENCE ANYWAY?

In summary, the doctrines of Mormonism that irreconcilably separate the Mormon Church and the Christian Church are as follows:

1. All churches except the Mormon Church are in error, all are abominations before God.

2. The Bible is, at best, a weak source of truth. It is in error and God has sent more complete and accurate scripture.

3. We must earn our own salvation.

4. We can become "Gods."

5. God was once a man but progressed into Godhood. So did our Heavenly Mother.

6. All this is known because God sent a prophet in the latter days.

These doctrines are not conceptual differences of the same man/God relationship. If they are truly the LDS theology, then Mormons and Christians are actually worshipping at different altars with totally different Gods and gospels!

Now the question is, **what do we do with this information?** If God is a loving and caring God, He will have provided some way for us to check out different gospels, different christs, and even different gods.

How can we, at such opposite ends in doctrinal difference, come together on some common ground to evaluate these differences in an effort to determine both truth and error?

THE COMMON DENOMINATOR

The one area upon which we agree is the Holy Bible being the Word of God (insofar as it is translated correctly).

And we do have the correct translation of the original scriptures. The Dead Sea scrolls verify that we have the correct translation of the Old Testament; and a huge mass of ancient manuscripts of the New Testament verify that our New Testament is the same text that was first given to the Church of Christ.

Since both the Christian and the Mormon basically believe that the Bible is God's Word to man through the age of the Apostles, let's see what it has to say regarding the subjects we have covered.

FIRST, A WARNING OR TWO

The Bible is explicit in its warnings regarding doctrines other than those given in detail by the New Testament writers. Let's look at a few. Remember, they pertain to warnings against teachings other than those THEY brought to the people.

> But I fear, lest by any means, as the serpent beguiled Eve through his subtlety, so your minds should be corrupted from the simplicity that is in Christ. For if he that cometh preacheth another Jesus, whom we have not preached, or if ye receive another spirit, which ye have not received, or another gospel, which ye have not accepted...

> For such are false apostles, deceitful workers, transforming themselves into the apostles of Christ. And no marvel; for Satan himself is transformed into an angel of light.

Therefore it is no great thing if his ministers also be transformed as the ministers of righteousness; whose end shall be according to their works. (2 Corinthians 11:3-4, 13-15)

I marvel that ye are so soon removed from him that called you into the grace of Christ unto another gospel: Which is not another; but there be some that trouble you, and would pervert the gospel of Christ.

But though we, or an angel from heaven, preach any other gospel unto you than that which we have preached unto you, let him be accursed. 1:9 As we said before, so say I now again, if any man preach any other gospel unto you than that ye have received, let him be accursed. (Galatians 1:6-9)

Just what was the gospel Paul preached to the early church?

Moreover, brethren, I declare unto you the gospel which I preached unto you, which also ye have received and wherein ye stand. By which also ye are saved, if ye keep in memory what I have preached unto you, unless ye have believed in vain.

For I delivered unto you first of all that which I also received, how that Christ died for our sins according to the scriptures; and that he was buried, and that he rose again the third day according to the scriptures. (1 Cor. 15:1-5.)

Preach the word; be instant in season, and out of season; reprove, rebuke, exhort with all long-suffering and doctrine. For the time will come when they will not endure sound doctrine, but after their own lusts, shall they heap to themselves teachers, having itching ears; And they shall turn away their ears from the truth, and shall be turned unto fables. (2 Timothy 4:2-4)

But there were false prophets also among the people, even as there shall be false teachers among you, who privily shall bring in damnable heresies, even denying the Lord that bought them, and bring upon themselves swift destruction. And many shall follow their pernicious ways; by reason of whom the way of truth shall be evil spoken of. (2 Peter 2:1-2)

And then if any man shall say to you, Lo, here is Christ; or, lo, he is there; believe him not: For false Christs and false prophets shall rise, and shall shew signs and wonders, to seduce, if it were possible, even the elect. But take ye heed: behold, I have foretold you all things. (Mark 13:21-23)

Now I beseech you, brethren, mark them which cause divisions and offences contrary to the doctrine which ye have learned; and avoid them. For they that are such serve not our Lord Jesus Christ, but their own belly; and by good words and fair speeches deceive the hearts of the simple. (Romans 16:17-18)

Beware of false prophets, which come to you in sheep's clothing, but inwardly they are ravening wolves. (Matthew 7:15)

Out of the mouths of two or three witnesses are all things proven true (Matthew 18:16). In the case of warnings about false doctrine and false prophets, I have more than doubled the number of two or three witnesses.

I am concerned that you come to know that Mormonism faces the grave danger of eternal condemnation if its doctrines are not in full accord with the Word of God.

A TRUE PROPHET?

James Talmage stated the challenge quite clearly in the book, *The Articles of Faith*.

The question of this man's [Joseph Smith] divine commission is a challenging one for the world today. If his claims to a divine appointment be false, forming as they do the foundation of the Church in this last dispensation, the superstructure cannot be stable; if however, his avowed ordination under the hands of heavenly personages be a fact, one need search no farther for the cause of the phenomenal vitality and continuous development of the restored church. *(The Articles of Faith, p.8)*

Joseph Smith, himself, put it all into boastful perspective when he said:

I have more to boast of than any man had. I am the only man that has been able to keep a whole church together since the days of Adam. A large majority of the whole have stood by me. Neither Paul, John, Peter nor Jesus ever did it.

> I boast that no man ever did such a work as I. The follow-
> ers of Jesus ran away from Him; but the Latter-day Saints
> never ran away from me yet. *(History of the Church, vol.6,
> pp.408-09, 1844)*

Brother Talmage, we accept the opportunity to test the Prophet Joseph Smith because upon his honor rests the honor of the Mormon gospel.

TESTS OF A PROPHET
The Word of God is amazingly clear in the testing of a prophet. Numerous scriptural tests are available, in detail and with enough backup scripture to confirm the validity of each test. Although there are many tests, we will limit ours to four areas.

TEST #1—OTHER GODS

> *If there arise among you a dreamer of dreams, and giveth
> thee a sign or a wonder, And the sign or the wonder come to
> pass, whereof he spake unto thee saying, let us go after other
> gods, which thou hast not known, and let us serve them;*
>
> *Thou shalt not hearken unto the words of that prophet, or
> that dreamer of dreams...and that prophet, or that dreamer
> of dreams shall be put to death. (Deuteronomy 13:1-5)*

A true prophet of God will not teach a conflicting doctrine of God. Not only does the Mormon doctrine of God (the Law of Eternal Progression) totally conflict with the basic scriptural God, but it is even in conflict with Mormonism's teachings.

First, the "official" version of the first vision is in major conflict with the "only known account of the vision in Joseph Smith's own hand," which was written about six years before the official account as recorded in *The Pearl of Great Price*. It states:

> ...the Lord heard my cry in the wilderness and while in
> the attitude of calling upon the Lord in **the 16th year** of
> my age a pillar of light above the brightness of the sun at
> noon day come down from above and rested upon me and
> I was filled with the spirit of god and **the Lord** opened the

> heavens upon me and *I saw the Lord* and he spake unto me saying Joseph my son thy sins are forgiven thee, go thy way walk in my statutes and keep my commandments behold I am the Lord of glory *I was crucifyed* for the world that all those who believe on my name may have Eternal life behold the world lieth in sin at this time and none doeth good no not one they have turned aside from the gospel and keep not my commandments they draw near to me with their lips while their hearts are far from me and mine anger is kindling against the inhabitants of the earth to visit them according to their ungodliness and to bring to pass that which hath been spoken by the mouths of the prophets and Apostles behold and lo I come quickly as it was written of me in the cloud clothed in the glory of *my Father.*

This account was taken from *BYU Studies*, Spring 1969, p.281. Dean C. Jessee, Church Historical Department states: "This is the only known account of the vision in his [Joseph Smith's] own hand." (*Dialogue: A Journal of Mormon Thought*, Spring 1971, p.86).

There was *no mention of God and Jesus in the flesh*, only Jesus in a vision into the Heavens.

Secondly, the God of Mormonism and the Law of Eternal Progression do not agree with *The Book of Mormon* spoken of as containing the "Fullness of the Everlasting Gospel" (*D&C* 27:5). **Nowhere** in its pages is there any reference to either the God of Mormonism or the Law of Eternal Progression. In fact, quite the opposite. One of the many Mormon scriptures that describes the nature of God is as follows:

> And now Abinadi said...I would that ye should understand that **God Himself** should come down among the children of men, and shall redeem his people, and because he dwelleth in the flesh he shall be called the Son of God and having subjected the flesh to the will of the Father, being the Father and the Son.

> The Father because He was conceived by the power of God; and the Son because of the flesh; thus becoming the

Father and the Son. And they are one god, ye the very eternal Father of heaven and earth.

And thus the flesh becoming subject to the spirit, or the Son to the Father, being one God. (*The Book of Mormon, Mosiah 15:1-5*)

TEST #2—FALSE PROPHECY

But the prophet, which shall presume to speak a word in my name, which I have not commanded him to speak, or that shall speak in the name of other Gods, even that Prophet shall die.

> *And if thou say in thine heart, How shall we know the word which the LORD hath not spoken? When a prophet speaketh in the name of the LORD, if the thing follow not, nor come to pass, that is the thing which the LORD hath not spoken, but the prophet hath spoken it presumptuously; thou shalt not be afraid of him. (Deuteronomy 18:20-22)*

A true prophet of God cannot utter a single false prophecy, **not one**! At no time can he give out a "Thus saith the Lord" and have it not come to pass. Joseph Smith gave forth approximately 64 prophecies. 64 times he said, "Thus saith the Lord."

If even **one single one of these prophecies failed** to come to pass, the scriptures call Joseph a false prophet. Some very comprehensive research has gone into this area. It is easy to do research on historical events. Out of 64 prophecies, **58 of them fail the test!** Only six of them came to pass!

Even granting the ability of the Mormon challenger to persuade the researcher to ignore or disregard 50 of them, the remaining eight still totally destroy (eight times) the honor of Joseph Smith as a prophet of the God of Abraham, of Moses and of John the Baptist.

Let's look at a few of these prophecies.

THE CIVIL WAR PROPHECY

Every Mormon should be familiar with the prophecy concerning the Civil War. But have you really looked at it in its entirety and checked it out?

1. Verily, **thus saith the Lord** concerning the wars that will **shortly come to pass,** beginning at the rebellion of South Carolina, which will eventually terminate in the death and misery of many souls;

2. And the time will come that war will be pour out upon all nations, beginning at this place.

3. For behold, the Southern States shall be divided against the Northern States, and the Southern States will call on other nations, even the nation of Great Britain...and they shall also call upon other nations, in order to defend themselves against other nations; **and then** war shall be poured out upon all nations.

4. And it shall come to pass, after many days, slaves shall rise up against their masters, who shall be marshalled and disciplined for war.

5. And it shall come to pass also that the remnants who are left of the land will marshal themselves, and shall become exceedingly angry, and shall vex the Gentiles with a sore vexation.

6. And thus, with the sword and by bloodshed the inhabitants of the earth shall mourn; and with famine, and plague, and earthquake, and the thunder of heaven, and the fierce and vivid lightning also, shall the inhabitants of the earth be made to feel the wrath and indignation, and chastening hand of an Almighty God until the consumption decreed hath made a full end of all nations.

7. That the cry of the saints, and the blood of the

saints, shall cease to come up into the ears of the Lord of Sabbath, from the earth, to be avenged of their enemies.

8. Wherefore, stand ye in holy places, and be not moved, until the day of the Lord come; for behold it cometh quickly, saith the Lord. Amen. (Doctrine and Covenants, p.87)

First, it was given on Christmas day, 1832, in appearance almost 30 years before the Civil War began. Yet, in actual fact, Congress had passed a tariff in July of 1832 that South Carolina declared unacceptable. Six months later, or during Christmas season, 1832, the nation's press expected and wrote about an immediate outbreak of Civil War to being with this South Carolina rebellion. Even the US Army was on alert in the matter. With this in mind, it was no great revelation to predict the events stated in verse #1.

In fact, however, the outbreak *did not* come to pass. The entire prophecy was shelved and never appeared in print during Joseph Smith's lifetime! The first two editions of the *History of the Church* did not include it even though it was in the handwritten manuscript. It did not appear in print until 1851, when the nation was again having problems between the north and the south.

Secondly, the scope of the prophecy is that the war would begin locally and pour out upon all nations, and *it shall be the direct cause* of an international global war. This is a definite prophecy that *DID NOT* come to pass at all.

Third, verses 3-6 state that the slaves shall rise up, the "remnants left in the land" shall come against the Gentiles (non-Mormons) and the bloodshed, famines, plagues (caused by this great war) shall bring, with God's wrath, "a full end of all nations." Again, a definite, tangible prophecy that *DID NOT* come to pass.

By any test, within any standard, the prophecy on the Civil War was and *is* a false prophecy.

THE GREASE SPOT PROPHECY

On 16 December 1843, Joseph Smith spoke of a petition he had filed with Congress for protection of the Latter-Day Saints:

> While discussing the petition with Congress, I prophesied by virtue of the Holy Priesthood vested in me, and in the name of the Lord Jesus Christ, that, if Congress will not hear our petition and grant us protection, they shall be broken up as a government, and God shall **damn** them and there shall nothing be left of them **not even a grease spot.** *(Millennial Star, vol.22, p.455)*

Needless to say, Congress did not grant the petition and the government grew to be the most powerful government in the world! Another false prophecy!

JESUS' RETURN

While Ezekiel and other prophets of old set the stage for specific events to unfold over the centuries, Joseph Smith was talking in the NOW times, not in the distant future. In 1835:

> President Smith then stated...it was the will of God that those who went to Zion, with a determination to lay down their lives, if necessary, would be ordained to the ministry, and go forth to prune the vineyard for the last time, for the **coming of the Lord** which was nigh, even fifty-six years should wind up the scene. *(History of the Church, vol.2, p.182.)*

He later added that if he met with a violent end, the scene would wind up a good ten years earlier. Well, 1881 and 1891 came and went without any return of Christ. Another specific test of exact prophecy and another failure.

WHO IS OLIVER GRANGER?

Just one of the simpler prophecies dealt with the great fame of one Oliver Granger.

> And again I say unto you, I remember my servant, Oliver Granger; behold, verily, I say unto him that his name shall be hand in sacred remembrance from generation to generation, forever and ever; saith the Lord. *(Doctrine and Covenants 117:12)*

Silly? Yes! Of great importance? No! False? Yes, unless you and three out of four Mormons you ask tell you with fond remembrance, just who Oliver Granger really was.

TEST #3—OUT OF HARMONY WITH OTHER "TRUE" PROPHETS?

> *To the law and to the testimony: If they speak not according to this Word, it is because there is no light in them. (Isaiah 8:20)*

Joseph Smith not only falls out of harmony with the Bible with his doctrines on God, but is also in disharmony with the Word of God in several other areas.

THE MORMON APOSTASY NOT SCRIPTURAL

Joseph Smith claims a total, complete apostasy took place. This, in spite of numerous scriptures promising that Christ shall come and establish His Church and it shall never be taken from us. Matthew 16:18 says:

> *And I say also unto thee, that thou art Peter [Petros = "little stone"], and upon this rock [Petra = Bedrock = Jesus] I will build my church and **the gates of hell shall not prevail against it**. [See 1 Cor.10:4 for the same use of the word "Rock"]*

THE MORMON PRIESTHOOD NOT SCRIPTURAL

The LDS Church teaches that Christ established the "true church" government before He ascended. Where is the establishment of the Melchizedek Priesthood? Where is the witness **of even one scripture** where Christ laid hands upon any man and ordained him to the Melchizedek or Aaronic Priesthood?

Further, where in the New Testament does Jesus confirm

the Old Testament Priesthood to be established order for His Church? Quite the opposite was actually true! (See Matthew 16:5-12)

In fact, John the Baptist, the man who Joseph Smith said came down from heaven and ordained him to the Aaronic Priesthood *NEVER* even had that authority! (See Matthew 21:23-27) If he did, the people who controlled the Aaronic Priesthood in those days surely didn't know about it!

Where in the New Testament does Christ establish temple ceremonies the rites and rituals, blood oaths, secret words, names, combinations? The wearing of specially designed and marked garments?

Where did He establish His 12 apostles to be under the control and direction of a prophet and his two counselors? Who was the first Prophet, Seer and Revelator so established? Where in the New Testament was he set apart and ordained as such?

Where did Jesus establish polygamy as the path to righteousness as the "New and Everlasting Covenant" with God?

If the Church Jesus established was "God's Perfect Church" (Mormon emphasis), how could Christ establish it *forever* and miss all these highly important items?

TEST #4—A LYING PROPHET

The ancient and honourable, he is the head; and the prophet that teacheth lies, he is the tail. For the leaders of this people cause them to err, and they that are led of them are destroyed. (Isaiah 9:15-16)

The LORD said unto me, the prophets prophesy lies in my name: I sent them not, neither have I commanded them, neither spake unto them: the prophesy unto you a false vision and divination, and a thing of naught, and the deceit of their heart. (Jeremiah 14:14)

Joseph Smith openly violated this trust many times. Two of the more significant times he knowingly lied while the

Prophet and spiritual leader of the LDS people are herein
mentioned. Both times, his position would have been in serious jeopardy had the real facts been known!

JOSEPH THE GLASS LOOKER

It was charged that Joseph Smith was accused and found
guilt of parting a local farmer from his money in a less than
honest scheme, commonly money digging or glass looking.
It was reported to have been an activity that brought him
rebuke from his soon-to-be father-in-law, Isaac Hale. It is also
historically recorded that he was removed from membership
in a local Methodist church because of the activity and trial
results.

Joseph Smith skims over the specific event leading to
the trial in *The Pearl of Great Price* (Joseph Smith History
1:56) explaining that he was only a day worker for the man
so engaged and not personally involved. Mormon writers
have continually challenged its doubters to find the records
(seemingly lost) and prove Joseph Smith a liar or stop the
attacks.

Mormon writer Hugh Nibley, in *The Myth Makers*, p.142,
says:

> If this court record is authentic it is the most damning evi-
> dence in existence against Joseph Smith.

Well, in spite of 140 years of silence, the records did turn
up. In 1971, Reverend Wesley Walters discovered them in the
basement of the Chenango County, New York jailhouse.

The records, affidavits, and other data show conclusively
that Joseph Smith was arrested, went to trial, was found guilty
as an imposter in the Stowell matter of "glass looking." It is
not a matter of debate, opinion or religious preference. It is a
proven historical fact.

The key issue here is NOT where he did or did not indulge

TO MORONI WITH LOVE

in the practice. The issue is that Joseph Smith **LIED** in the matter.

JOSEPH THE POLYGAMIST

In the 1835 edition of the *Doctrine and Covenants*, the issue of polygamy was very definitely spoken out against.

> Inasmuch as this "Church of Christ" has been reproached with the crime of fornication and polygamy; we declare that we believe that one man should have one wife; and one woman but one husband; except that in the event of death when either is at liberty to marry again. *(Doctrine and Covenants 101:4, 1835 edition)*

In other words, no man could marry a second wife unless the first one died. No divorce and no polygamy. It was labeled a CRIME! That was the "Word" from God.

However, Joseph Smith didn't exactly live as he preached. In 1887, Andrew Jenson, Mormon Church Historian, listed 27 women who were married to Joseph Smith, *officially*, during the time such a union was a "crime" before God.

Fawn Brodie, in her book, *No Man Knows My History*, (Appendix C) lists each in detail and brings the number *to a total of 48 women* who were sealed to the Prophet and united with him in "Holy Polygamy." These marriages are not to be confused with later "proxy" sealings to the dead Joseph Smith. 149 additional dead women were later sealed to him in temple ceremonies, according to Brodie.

It was only when it became so openly known that Smith finally admitted it and declared it a special gift of God and released the now "scripturized" law of polygamy given in *Doctrine and Covenants* §132. Although this "revelation" came forth in 1843, it not show up in "scripture" until 1876. The earlier warning against polygamy (*Doctrine and Covenants* 101:4, 1835 edition) just disappeared without not or explanation.

It should be noted that Joseph's new "revelation" giving

God's sanction for what was a crime before Him only a few years earlier, DID NOT retroactively absolve Joseph of all wrong. *Doctrine and Covenants* 132:61 states.

> If any man espouse a virgin and desire to espouse another, and the first give her consent, and if he espouse the second, they are virgins, and have vowed to no other man, then is he justified; he cannot commit adultery for they are given unto him; for he cannot commit adultery with that that belongeth unto him and to no one else.

First, Joseph had already been quite active in the "espousing" business long before his wife heard of the doctrine, long before she reluctantly gave consent to be party to it.

Second, seven of the ten wives he already had *were already married to other living men* in complete opposition to the new "revelation" Joseph received! Joseph received "Marriage for eternity, with concubinal privileges" while the husbands had married for "time only."

Third, notwithstanding the problems already stated, the whole idea of multiple wives was (and still is) in total disagreement with *Doctrine and Covenants* 42:22 which says, "Thou shalt love thy WIFE with all thy heart, and shall cleave unto HER and NONE else." (Author's emphasis)

A LIE IS A LIE

Friends, a lie is a lie is a lie, and when it comes out of the mouth of a man proclaimed to be a prophet of God, that man is sent not of God, neither has God commanded him. He speaks only out of "the deceit of his heart." (Jeremiah 14:14)

JOSEPH THE FALSE PROPHET

I beseech you to seek further in the Word of God, the Bible, to test all things by it and through it. The salvation Joseph Smith taught is not of the Lord. He has led you to follow after other gods and he has led you away from the true Word of God into false scripture.

MORMONISM, AS THE "ONLY TRUE CHURCH," CANNOT BE PARTIALLY TRUE! IT MUST BE TOTALLY CORRECT OR TOTALLY WRONG. IT IS MY TESTIMONY TO YOU THAT IT IS TOTALLY WRONG!

You may look about you in a Sacrament Meeting and find my words harsh and difficult to accept among all the smiling, radiant faces. But Satan is not going to come to you looking like a 14-foot frog with hair and fire coming out of his nostrils. He is going to look just like an "angel of light" and so will his ministers (2 Corinthians 11:14-15).

My heart weeps because the scriptures are clear in the warnings as to the end of those who follow such prophets and their ministers.

> *For the leaders of this people cause them to err; and they that are led of them are destroyed. (Isaiah 9:16)*

MORMONISM AND CHRISTIANITY COMPARED

AS A MORMON, ARE YOU WILLING to stake your eternal destination on the doctrines outlined below? I have taken the basic doctrines that separate Mormonism and orthodox Christianity and made a simple comparison. You deserve to know the facts about the true doctrines of the Mormon Church, the Church of Jesus Christ of Latter-day Saints. I Invite you to check out each quotation in its full context.

MORMONISM'S GOD WAS ONCE A MAN

> "God himself was one as we are now, and is an exalted man... I say, if you were to see him today, you would see him like a man in form... like yourselves in all the person, image, and very form as a man... He was once a man like us; yea, that God himself, the Father of us all, dwelt on an earth." *(Joseph Smith, History of the Church, Vol. 6, p. 305.)*

THE BIBLE:

God was never a man. He created man! God has been God from all eternity to all eternity. (Psalm 41:13, 90:2, 102:25-27; Romans 1:22-23)

MORMONISM'S GOD IS LIMITED

"The universe is filled with vast numbers of intelligences, and we further learn that Elohim is God simply because all of these intelligences honor and sustain him as such... if He should ever do anything to violate the confidence or "sense of justice" of these intelligences, they would promptly withdraw their support, and the "power" of God would disintegrate. He would cease to be God." W. Cleon Skousen *(Former BYU Professor & founder of Mormon-based National Center For Constitutional Studies, The First 2000 Years, p. 355)*

"The Father has a body of flesh and bones as tangible as mans," *(Doctrine and Covenants, 130:22)*

"If God possesses a form, that form is of necessity of definite proportions, and therefore of limited extension and space. It is impossible for Him to occupy at one time more than one space of such limits." *(James E. Talmage, Articles of Faith, page 43)*

THE BIBLE:

God is infinite! Any other "god" is a false god. (2 Chronicles 6:18; Psalm 139:4-8; Jeremiah 23:24)

MRS. GOD?

"In the heaven where our spirits were born, there are many Gods, each of whom has his own wife or wives, which were given to him ... while yet in his mortal state." *(Orson Pratt ,Apostle, The Seer, p. 37)*

"This doctrine that there is a Mother in Heaven was affirmed in all plainness by the First Presidency of the Church." *(Bruce R. McConkie, Apostle, Mormon Doctrine, p. 516)*

THE BIBLE:

Absolutely no mention of any "wives" of God! (Matthew 22:29,30)

NO VIRGIN BIRTH

"Christ was begotten by an Immortal Father in the same way that mortal men are begotten by mortal fathers... Christ was born into the world as the literal Son of this Holy Being; he was born in the same personal, real and literal sense that any mortal son is born to a mortal father." *(McConkie, Mormon Doctrine, pp. 547, 742)*

THE BIBLE:

Jesus was begotten by the Holy Ghost. Mary was indeed a virgin right up to the Lord's birth. (Matthew 1:18-23; Luke 1:35)

MORMONISM'S JESUS AND SATAN ARE BROTHERS

"The appointment of Jesus to be the Savior of the world was contested by one of the other sons of God. He was called Lucifer - this spirit-brother of Jesus desperately tried to become the Savior of mankind." *(Milton R. Hunter, The Gospel Through the Ages, p. 15)*

THE BIBLE:

The real JESUS is the only begotten Son and is God the Son (John 1:1-14). Satan was a created angel, not a son of God (Isaiah 14:12). Jesus created all things and in Him the fullness of God dwells! (Colossians 1:15-20; Philippians 2:5-11; Hebrews 1:1-13)

MORMONISM'S JESUS WAS MARRIED

"Jesus was the bridegroom at the marriage of Cana of Galilee. We say it was Jesus Christ who was married... whereby he could see his seed." *(Orson Hyde, Apostle, Journal of Discourses, Vol. 2, p. 82)*

THE BIBLE:

NO! Check out John 2:1-12! This LDS doctrine is generally not taught openly today. However, since marriage in a LDS temple is mandatory to progress to become a god in Mormonism, to fit the theology of Mormonism, the LDS "Jesus" has to be married. Otherwise He would only be a ministering servant to those in Mormonism's heaven who have "celestial marriage."

AUTHORITY OF THE BIBLE DENIED

"Ignorant translators, careless transcribers, or designing and corrupt priests have committed many errors — many plain and precious things were deleted, in consequence of which error and falsehood poured into the churches. One of the great heresies of modern Christendom is the unfounded assumption that the Bible contains all of the inspired teachings now extant among men." *(McConkie, Mormon Doctrine, pp. 82,83)*

THE BIBLE:

The Bible says of itself that God's Word therein will stand forever (Isaiah 40:8; I Peter 1:25). Ask any Mormon leader to show you exactly where the errors exist. Most of these doctrines added by Mormonism are not in the Book of Mormon, either (said to contain the "fullness of the everlasting gospel")!

MORMONISM SAYS ALL OUR CHURCHES ARE FALSE

"I was answered that I must join none of them, for they were all wrong; and the personage who addressed me said that all their creeds were an abomination in his sight; and those professors were all corrupt." *(Joseph Smith, Pearl of Great Price, 2:19)*

"This Church is the only true and living church upon the face of the whole earth." *(Doctrine and Covenants 1:30)*

"There is no salvation outside the Church of Jesus Christ of Latter-day Saints." McConkie, Mormon Doctrine, p. 670. "All other churches are entirely destitute of all authority from God; and any person who receives Baptism or the Lord's Supper from their hands will highly offend God; for He looks upon them as the most corrupt of all people. Both Catholics and Protestants are nothing less than the whore of Babylon." *(Orson Pratt, The Seer, p. 255)*

THE BIBLE:

The CHURCH is the spiritual body of Christians with Jesus at its head. That is the true church, not an organization! (Ephesians 1:22-23, 4:11-16; I Corinthians 1:2, 12:12; Matthew 16:18).

WHAT JOSEPH SMITH SAID OF HIMSELF

"I have more to boast of than ever any man had. I am the only man that has ever been able to keep a whole church together since the days of Adam. A large majority of the whole have stood by me. Neither Paul, John, Peter, nor Jesus ever did it. I boast that no man ever did such a work as I. The followers of Jesus ran away from Him; but the Latter-day Saints never ran away from me yet." *(Joseph Smith, History of the Church, Vol 6, pp.408,409)*

THE BIBLE:

No prophet of God ever spoke like that. Are you trusting your eternal salvation in a system set up by this man. In Daniel 4:28-33, King Nebuchadnezzar had such pride and was driven out by God to live with the animals . Just one month after delivering the above speech, Joseph Smith was killed by a mob (but only after he had shot and killed two of the mob). *(History of the Church, Vol. 7, pp. 102,103)*

MORMON LEADERS' VIEW OF THEMSELVES

"When our leaders speak, the thinking as been done. When they point the way, there is no other which is safe. When they give direction, it should mark the end of controversy." *(Improvement Era, Official LDS church magazine, June 1945, p. 345)*

"The living Prophet is more vital to us than the Standard Works (Bible, Book of Mormon, etc.). The living Prophet is more important to us than a dead prophet (David, Moses, Isaiah, etc.). Those who would remove prophets from politics would take God out of government." *(LDS prophet, Ezra Taft Benson, address at Brigham Young University, Feb. 26, 1980)*

THE BIBLE:

In these last days God speaks through His Son (Hebrews 1:1-2). The authority claimed by the Mormon Church is through an "Aaronic Priesthood," which cannot be valid since Jesus abolished it, as He took its place (Hebrews 7:11-19, 8:6-13); and a "Melchizedek Priesthood" which never existed as any operative "priesthood." Jesus is our only High Priest. He alone holds this permanently and no one else! (Hebrews 7:15-28, 9:11-15).

AFRICAN RACE WAS CURSED

"Not only was Cain called upon to suffer, but because of his wickedness, he became the father of an inferior race. A curse was placed upon him and that curse has been continued through his lineage and must do so while time endures. Millions of souls have come into this world cursed with a black skin and have been denied the privilege of Priesthood and the fullness of the blessings of the Gospel." Joseph *(Fielding Smith, Prophet, The Way To Perfection, p. 102.)*

"You see some classes of the human family that are black, uncouth, uncomely, disagreeable and low in their habits, wild, and seemingly deprived of nearly all the blessings of the intelligence that is generally bestowed upon mankind." *(Brigham Young, Prophet, Journal of Discourses, Vol. 7, p. 290)*

"Shall I tell you the law of God in regard to the African race? If the white man... mixes his blood with the seed of Cain, the penalty, under the law of God, is death on the spot. This will always be so." *(B. Young, Journal of Discourses, Vol. 10, p. 110)*

While the LDS god "forgave" blacks in June, 1978, their firm doctrine still is that this whole race of people are "cursed with a black skin" for sins committed by them before they were born.

The new revelation announced that worthy blacks could now receive the privileges of the LDS priesthood and secret temple rites like the whites. May all true Christians flee from such hypocrisy!

COUNCIL IN HEAVEN

"The head God called together the Gods and sat in grand council to bring forth the world... In the beginning, the head of the Gods called a council of the gods; and they came together and concocted a plan to create the world and people it." *(Joseph Smith, Teachings of the Prophet Joseph Smith, pp. 348, 349)*

"The contention in heaven was... Jesus said there would be certain souls that would not be saved; and the Devil said he could save them all, and laid his plans before the grand council, who gave their vote in favour of Jesus Christ. So the Devil rose up in rebellion against God, and was cast down, with all who put up their heads for him." *(Joseph Smith, Journal of Discourses, Vol. 6, page 8)*

JOSEPH SMITH WILL SIT IN JUDGMENT

"No man or woman in this dispensation will ever enter into the celestial kingdom of God without the consent of Joseph Smith. From the day that the Priesthood was taken from the earth to the winding up scene of all things, every man and woman must have the certificate of Joseph Smith, junior, as a passport to their entrance into the mansion where God and Christ are." *(Brigham Young, Journal of Discourses, Vol. 7, p. 289).*

"If we get our salvation, we shall have to pass by him; if we enter our glory, it will be through the authority he has received. We cannot get around him." *(President George Q. Cannon, quoted in 1988, Melchizedek Priesthood Study Guide, p. 142)*

LDS PERFORM RESURRECTIONS

"If we ask who will stand at the head of the resurrection in this last dispensation, the answer is — Joseph Smith, Junior, the Prophet of God. He is the man who will be resurrected and receive the keys of the resurrection, and he will seal this authority upon others, and they will hunt up their friends and resurrect them." *(Discourses of Brigham Young, p. 116)*

SAVIORS OF THE DEAD

"We are the only people that know how to save our progenitors, how to save ourselves, and how to save our posterity in the celestial kingdom of God; that we are the people God has chosen by whom to establish his kingdom and introduce correct principles into the world; and that we are in fact the saviours of the world..." *(John Taylor, Prophet, Journal of Discourses, Vol. 6, p. 163)*

SUN AND MOON INHABITED

"Nearly all the great discoveries of men in the last half century have, in one way or another... contributed to prove Joseph Smith to be a prophet. As far back as 1837, I know that he said the moon was inhabited by men and women the same as this earth, and that they lived to a greater age than we do — that they live generally to near the age of a 1000 years, He described the men as averaging near six feet in height, and dressing quite uniformly in something near the Quaker style." *(O. B. Huntington, Young Women's Journal, Vol. 3, p. 264, 1892)*

"Who can tell us of the inhabitants of this little planet that shines of an evening, called the moon?... So it is with regard to the inhabitants of the sun. Do you think it is inhabited? I rather think it is. Do you think there is any life there? No question of it" *(B. Young, Journal of Discourses, Vol. 13, p. 271).*

TOTAL PERFECTION DEMANDED

"We also have to forsake the sin and never repeat it, not even in our minds... In order to remain forgiven, we must never commit the sin again." *(Uniform System for Teaching Families, pp.35,36)*

"In other words, If there is one divine law that he does not keep he is barred from participating in the Kingdom, and figuratively guilty of all, since he is denied all." *(Joseph Fielding Smith, Prophet, Answers to Gospel Questions, Vol.3, p. 26)*

SOUND DIFFERENT?

As unbelievable as it may seem, the above information is actual LDS doctrine. The quotations have not been taken out of context. LDS prophets have taught such things and are believed speak for God.

As a former Mormon who once sincerely believed in and staked my life on these doctrines, we assure you that they are accurately stated. This is given to you because you deserve to have the facts. Millions of dollars can create any image through Readers' Digest ads and slick television commercials, but the doctrines of Mormonism are NOT Christian.

**Mormonism
is a counterfeit faith with:
A different "Jesus"—
A different "God"—
A different "Gospel"!**

TO THE MORMON

This information has been given to you in love. I assure you that it is accurate and honest. The programs, and certainly the people of the Mormon Church are good. However, you can have the greatest organization, and a sincere faith, but if that organization directs your faith to a "god" who is not the one and only true God of the Bible, but rather a false god who cannot save, then after your own death, that organization and that faith will save you from nothing.

Take up the challenge! Dare to question and become a genuine seeker of the truth. Were you given the information on the "meat" of Mormonism, which I have outlined here, during the missionary lessons before you joined the church? Were you asked to make an eternal decision, based upon incomplete and inaccurate information? I URGE YOU to call out to the One True God of Abraham, Isaac, and Jacob to reveal Himself to you and to ask the One True Jesus to apply His sacrifice on the cross to your sins personally! There is no other God and no other say!

A PERSONAL TESTIMONY

THIS WITNESS IS NOT GIVEN TO hurt you. It is given to testify to you that the Lord loved me as much when I was a Mormon as he loves me today; that He loves you every bit as much as He loves me, but that He weeps for every soul lost in false doctrines and false religions. This is not some intellectual battle between us; for the battle is the Lord's, and it is with powers outside the realm of flesh and blood. He is calling His own from the world. He stands at the door and knocks. He has NO prophets and priests waiting there ahead of Him…He stands there!

Dear brothers and sisters, Joseph Smith has led you back into the bondage of the Old Testament Law, and more than that, back under the control of a false prophet. Jesus Christ came to fulfill the Law. The New Covenant Lamb of God put an end to it all and replaced it with His love and intercession. JESUS is my high priest after the order of Melchizedek and there is *no other* in the kingdom of God (Hebrews 7:24).

Having left the Mormon Church after almost 20 years, it is my personal testimony to you that:

1. I do not place my eternal life in the hands of any Latter-Day Prophet nor is it (my eternal life) conditional on my membership in any church or priesthood. I place my life at the foot of the cross, in Jesus Christ and in God's Holy Word, the Bible.

2. Joseph Smith was not a prophet of God. He fails every test of a prophet, including teaching false doctrine, uttering false prophecies and lying.

3. The LDS Church is **NOT** "The Restored Gospel." Scripture promises and history proves that the "Gospel" never left the earth.

4. The Book of Mormon is manifestedly a contrived document and not of divine origin.

5. The Pearl of Great Price (particularly the Book of Abraham) is a work of pure fraud.

6. The Doctrine and Covenants have been rewritten, added to, and whole sections deleted in such proportion as to make it invalid as scripture of any kind, even if it were true that God originally spoke to Joseph Smith (which He didn't).

7. The LDS Church leadership has made serious and substantial changes to all their scriptures as well as most Church history. I believe they have done this in order to dupe their members, to hide doctrinal errors and to protect some leaders from exposure of their moral failure.

8. The Priesthood of the LDS Church holds absolutely NO authority to act in the name of GOD. Its origin is a lie and its power is the power of priestcraft, and its author is Satan.

9. The LDS Law of Eternal Progression with its unscriptural description of the **True Nature of God** is the real abomination in the sight of God.

It is my solemn testimony and firm belief that the Church of Jesus Christ of Latter-day Saints fails every test God has given us for this purpose.

As mentioned earlier, the Saviour foretold of this happening in Mark 13:21-22:

> And then if any man shall say to you, Lo, here is Christ; or, lo, he is there; believe him not: For false Christs and false prophets shall rise, and shall shew signs and wonders, to seduce, if it were possible, even the elect.

I chose to take heed to His Word in the 21st verse. "I believed them not." After my own evaluation, I determined that they were false prophets with a false christ and I had my name removed from the records of the LDS Church.

THE REAL JESUS

The real Jesus is waiting to love you and nurture you and lead you into the safety of His Word. It is no strange doctrine, but a **COMPLETE** doctrine, to submit yourself to the gentleness of the true Saviour.

Ask Him into your heart today! The Real Jesus, the one who died on Calvary for your sins. Believe on Him, believe that having Jesus of Nazareth as your Lord and Saviour is all that you need to live with your Heavenly Father; that you don't need church membership or a special priesthood or temple garments or a prophet to guide you...just JESUS! He is every that God could give.

> *I am crucified with Christ: nevertheless I live; yet not I, but Christ liveth in me: and the life which I now live in the flesh I live by the faith of the Son of God, who loved me, and gave himself for me. (Galatians 2:20)*

Ask Him into your life right now. He stands at the door of your heart and knocks!

For further information, contact Ed Decker, Saints Alive in Jesus at ed@SaintsAlive.com or visit our website at www.SaintsAlive.com.

ABOUT THE AUTHOR

Ed Decker has meticulously studied Mormonism for 45 years and implores readers to take a look into the basic doctrines of Mormonism.

He is the founder and International Director of Saints Alive in Jesus, a ministry that actively brings the gospel of grace to those lost in the darkness of cultic bondage. An accredited, long time Christian apologist, he is the author of such books as *The God Makers, Decker's Complete Handbook on Mormonism, Fast Facts on False Teachings, Understanding Islam* and *The Question of Freemasonry.*

For over 30 years, Ed has been an active speaker and teacher, traveling throughout the world working with churches of every Christian denomination. He personally conducts equipping sessions with pastors and lay workers and speaks at conferences in many nations. His ministry extends to radio, television, Christian documentary films and national talk shows.

Ed is a retired pastor and regularly visits hospitals and homes to pray for the sick, counseling and encouraging the body of Christ.

MORE BOOKS FROM ED DECKER

THE QUESTION OF FREEMASONRY
by ED DECKER

Ed's expanded edition of the small book that rocked Masonry. This is one to read and give to your pastor. Masonry is one of the most volatile subjects in the Christian church today. Ed Decker has carefully researched and studied the issues, doctrines and practices of Freemasonry. This booklet is an essential tool in understanding the challenge of a pagan invasion that has infiltrated the core of Christianity itself.

Perfect Bound, 5x8, 40 Pages, $5.00
ISBN# 1-60039-181-8

TO HELP YOU REVEAL THE TRUTH!

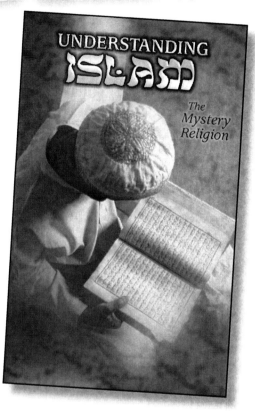

UNDERSTANDING ISLAM
by ED DECKER

On September 11, 2001, a group of terrorists—in the name of Islam—hijacked four passenger airliners and crashed them into select targets, killing thousands, and wounding thousands more. It was a monumental wake up call for America and for all of Christianity.

It's time we stop kidding ourselves. Either we are dealing with a group of extremist radicals, or Islam is a religion which breeds and incites its staunchest believers to act out the core tenets of its belief system.

Perfect Bound, 5x8, 44 Pages, $5.00
ISBN# 1-60039-180-X

TO ORDER, VISIT WWW.LAMPPOSTPUBS.COM

CPSIA information can be obtained at www.ICGtesting.com
Printed in the USA
LVOW06s0930140414

381601LV00009B/92/P